Discovering Global Missions

EXPLORE GOD'S HEART FOR THE NATIONS

DAVE GUILES

V4-0218

Discovering Global Missions
Explore God's Heart for the Nations

ISBN: 978-0-9978640-6-9
eISBN: 978-0-9978640-7-6
Published by Encompass World Publishing, Atlanta, GA 30362
the publishing arm of Encompass World Partners
EncompassWorldPartners.org

Written by Dave Guiles
Edited by John Ward, Deb Dunlevy, Bill Palmateer
Design and Layout by Evangela Creative (evangela.com)

Printed in U.S.A.

ABOUT THE SERIES

THE PATH: NAVIGATING THE JOURNEY TO GLOBAL MISSIONS

Travel tools and resources help us learn about destinations, give us insights, and point the way. Likewise, the titles in this series act as a map, a guide, and a compass to help you navigate the journey to global missions.

Start down the path to knowing God's heart for the nations and how you can become a part of his global mission.

Next steps on the path for those who are mobilizing individuals and teams into meaningful ministry to the nations.

Next steps on the path for potential cross-cultural workers discerning the call to making disciples among the nations.

ABOUT THE AUTHOR

DAVE GUILES grew up in the home of a church planter and pastor. In 1987, upon completing his Master of Divinity studies at *Grace Theological Seminary* (Winona Lake, IN), Dave and his wife, Sue, joined the staff of *Grace Brethren International Missions* (since renamed *Encompass World Partners*). Their primary ministry was church planting in Argentina, and Dave also served as Regional Coordinator for Latin America. He was the principal author of ACTS (the *Apostolic Church-planting Team Strategy*), as well as a series of creative evangelistic and discipleship methods and materials.

In April 2000, Dave and Sue returned to the USA so he could assume the role of Executive Director of Encompass. In the quest to retool a 100 +/- year-old mission agency for a rapidly-changing world, Dave led through a series of significant changes, including rebranding, relocation and restructuring of global operations. In addition to his role as Encompass' Executive Director, he also serves as Coordinator for the *Charis Alliance*, a global network of churches that share a common commitment to biblical truth, biblical relationships and biblical missions.

In 2013, Dave completed his Doctor of Ministry degree in missions at *Trinity Evangelical Divinity School* (Deerfield, IL). Dave and Sue currently reside near the Encompass World Partners' headquarters in Atlanta, and in the margins of a busy life are committed to helping start new churches.

ABOUT THE AGENCY

ENCOMPASS WORLD PARTNERS was birthed in 1900 from a commitment to make disciples among all nations.

Its purpose is: To mobilize, equip, deploy and nurture multinational teams of disciple-makers who live and proclaim the good news of Jesus Christ through engaging in sacrificial service, intentional evangelism and whole-life discipleship, resulting in the creation of healthy spiritual communities (churches).

The rallying cry of Encompass World Partners is *more fruitful disciple-making teams among the least-reached peoples of our world.* Learn more about the ministries of Encompass and how you can become involved at EncompassWorldPartners.org.

AUDCO VALVES

TABLE OF CONTENTS

聯發電器行
HITACHI
Panasonic
瑞興麻雀公司
富榮大押
FU WING PAWNSHOP
TAXI
的士
TAXI
CAMBODIA
SINGAPORE
Kuala Lumpur

INTRODUCTION

DISCOVERING GLOBAL MISSIONS

WELCOME TO AN EXCITING OPPORTUNITY to explore God's heart for his world and how you can become a part of his global mission. Through this book we trust you will gain deep insight and understanding of the task of making disciples, the necessity to go, the importance of nations, and how you can get involved.

Discovering global missions is a starting point in a journey that we hope you'll continue as you follow Jesus. **This book is part of a series of books called The Path, which are designed to help you navigate the journey to global missions.** At the conclusion of this book you'll be challenged to apply what you've learned in tangible ways and you'll be asked to consider taking the next step. This book is **the map** that allows you to get oriented as you start on your journey.

You may be going through this book on your own, with a missions mentor, or with a group, but it's important to note that it's *best expressed and applied in the context of a local church*. We believe that you don't have global missions without the local church and you don't have the local church without global missions. It sounds confusing, but by Chapter 3 you'll know what we mean, and in Chapter 4 you'll be encouraged to discover the opportunities your church is creating to help you engage in meaningful ways.

Each chapter includes a short video that will challenge and inspire you as you explore global missions. You will be exposed to a lot of scripture throughout the book, and we encourage you to answer all the questions for discussion. We pray that your heart for God's global mission will grow and that you'll respond in faith as you follow Jesus.

CHAPTER ONE

ONE PRIORITY

OVERVIEW:

The Bible is the story of God revealing his glory to all mankind. He invites us into that story by commissioning us to make disciples of Jesus Christ among all nations. When we make disciples among peoples who are different than ourselves, we are engaging in ***missions***. This chapter lays the foundation for understanding missions by exploring what's involved in ***making disciples***.

VIDEO **bit.ly/BiblicalBasisForMissions**

Questions for Discussion:

1. What did you like about the video?
2. What did you learn that is new to you?

INTRODUCTION:

This short video does an excellent job helping us understand how the Bible is the story of a God who is on mission. From Genesis to Revelation, we witness the wisdom, power and patience of a holy God who is *"not wishing that any should perish, but that all should reach repentance"* (2 Peter 3:9). We encourage you to review the

video again, and to look up the many Bible references included in it.

Now that we've established a clearer understanding of God's global mission, we turn to the important matter of what he expects from us. We'll closely examine some of the final words Jesus spoke, using them as a basic outline:

> *Go therefore and make disciples of all nations, baptizing them in the name of the Father and of the Son and of the Holy Spirit, teaching them to observe all that I have commanded you. And behold, I am with you always, to the end of the age.*
>
> **Jesus, quoted in Matthew 28:19,20**

It's worth noting that in the original language of the New Testament, *make disciples* is the only action word that appears in the form of an imperative command. Three additional verbs support this command by explaining actions that must accompany it: *going*, *baptizing* and *teaching them to observe*. Therefore, it makes sense for us to begin by exploring the command to *make disciples*. What is a disciple, and how are disciples made?

1. WHAT IS A DISCIPLE?

This question requires that we dig a bit deeper into the original language and the social context into which these words were spoken. The word *disciple* can be translated *learner* or *follower*. In the region where Jesus lived and ministered, it was commonly used to refer to a student who would attach himself to a master teacher. Please don't think in terms of the casual teacher-student relationships common in our schools today! This was a serious commitment, somewhat like the special relationship between an apprentice and a master artisan. One big difference, however, is that Jesus expects this relationship to be *permanent*.

For more than three years, Jesus invested heavily in the training of the first disciples. As he prepared to return to his Father, he instructed those disciples to make more disciples among all the nations of the world. They would face many obstacles in their quest to complete this command, some of which we'll examine later. For now, let's focus on the primary challenge: how could they connect new disciples with Jesus when he was no longer physically present?

The answer is found in their teaching and writings, which are collected together in what we call the New Testament. The books of Matthew, Mark, Luke and John record the story of Jesus' life, and illustrate how Jesus made disciples. The Acts of the Apostles and the Letters of the Apostles show how his early disciples fanned out into the known world to make more disciples of Christ.

QUESTIONS FOR DISCUSSION:

After Jesus returned to the Father, those who heard his command to make disciples went to extreme measures to obey him. They were willing to endure hardships, make great sacrifices, and even face torturous deaths at the hands of those who opposed their message. What do you think would motivate men and women to this level of obedience?

2. WHAT MOTIVATES US TO MAKE DISCIPLES?

Consider the disciples' final encounter with the risen Christ:

> *Now the eleven disciples went to Galilee, to the mountain to which Jesus had directed them. And when they saw him they worshiped him, but some doubted. And Jesus came and said to them, "All authority in heaven and on earth has been given to me. Go therefore and make disciples of all nations..."*
>
> **Matthew 28:16–19**

These verses appear directly before our key passage. Did you take note of what the early disciples did when they came face to face with the risen Christ? They fell to their knees and worshipped him. Jesus responded by acknowledging his right to be worshipped (*"All authority in heaven and on earth has been given to me."*) and followed immediately with the command to make more worshippers (*"Go therefore and make disciples of all nations..."*).

The greatest single motivation for making disciples arises from our acknowledgement that Jesus is Lord. When we make more disciples, we are simply inviting others to become worshippers of Jesus (which makes them worshippers of the true God).

But there are additional truths that played an important role in helping the early disciples embrace the command to make disciples of all nations. Let's look at them in more depth, quoting from the disciples' own words:

God is holy, and requires that mankind share his holiness.

> *This is the message we have heard from him and proclaim to you, that God is light, and in him is no darkness at all.*
>
> **1 John 1:5**

> *But as he who called you is holy, you also be holy in all your conduct, since it is written, "You shall be holy, for I am holy."*
>
> **1 Peter 1:15,16**

Mankind is separated from God because of his sin.

> *None is righteous, no, not one; no one understands; no one seeks for God. All have turned aside; together they have become worthless; no one does good, not even one."*
>
> **Romans 3:10–12**

> *For the wages of sin is death...*
>
> **Romans 6:23**

Yet God is love, and he seeks to restore mankind to a relationship with himself.

> *For God so loved the world, that he gave his only Son, that whoever believes in him should not perish but have eternal life.*
>
> **John 3:16**

Through Jesus Christ, God provides a way to reconcile man to himself .

> *Jesus said to him, "I am the way, and the truth, and the life. No one comes to the Father except through me.*
>
> **John 14:6**

> *And this is the testimony, that God gave us eternal life, and this life is in his Son. Whoever has the Son has life; whoever does not have the Son of God does not have life.*

1 John 5:11,12

One day, all mankind will be judged based upon how they respond to Jesus Christ.

> *For the wages of sin is death, but the free gift of God is eternal life in Christ Jesus our Lord.*
>
> **Romans 6:23**

> *This is evidence of the righteous judgment of God ... when the Lord Jesus is revealed from heaven with his mighty angels in flaming fire, inflicting vengeance on those who do not know God and on those who do not obey the gospel of our Lord Jesus. They will suffer the punishment of eternal destruction, away from the presence of the Lord and from the glory of his might, when he comes on that day to be glorified in his saints, and to be marveled at among all who have believed, because our testimony to you was believed.*
>
> **2 Thessalonians 1:5, 7–10**

The five important truths listed above form a short outline of the essence of the gospel message. *Gospel* simply means *good news*. What happens when we believe and act upon these truths? First, we come to see that the death, burial and resurrection of Jesus Christ really is good news. Second, it places upon us the obligation and urgency to share this good news with others.

> *Since, then, we know what it is to fear the Lord, we try to persuade others.*
>
> **2 Corinthians 5:11a**

QUESTIONS FOR DISCUSSION:

Take a moment to consider these five important truths. If we removed any one of them from the list, how might it impact our motivation to make disciples?

2. HOW DO WE MAKE DISCIPLES?

The five truths we just reviewed are very important, but they don't provide a complete picture of what it means to make disciples. They are just the starting point.

Why?

A. Because of the full meaning of the word disciple. Jesus doesn't simply invite us to believe certain truths, he invites us into a relationship with himself.

And this is eternal life, that they know you, the only true God, and Jesus Christ whom you have sent.

Jesus, quoted in John 17:3

FAST FACTS

Identifying as an *evangelical* simply means that we place ourselves within the group of Christians who believe in 1) the authority of the Bible as God's Word, 2) the literal death and resurrection of Jesus Christ, 3) the requirement that mankind respond in faith, and 4) our obligation to share this message with others.

Since 1900, the number of evangelical Christians worldwide has grown from 81 million to more than 400 million. To what do we attribute most of this growth? God has blessed the sacrifice of churches that send missionaries and the fruit of those missionaries, who have taken seriously the command to make disciples of all nations.

B. Because of the full meaning of our key passage. Note how two of the supporting verbs help flesh out what it means to make disciples.

Baptizing them in the name of the Father and of the Son and of the Holy Spirit...

Ever since Jesus gave this command, the physical act of entering water to be baptized has served as a visible way to proclaim our allegiance to the Father, Son and Holy Spirit. Baptism should be one of the first actions taken by a new disciple.

Teaching them to observe all that I have commanded you.

While baptism is a one-time act of obedience, these words point out how a disciple commits to a lifetime of obedience. After all, how long will it take us to know and put into practice everything that Jesus instructed us to do?

WORTH PONDERING:

Does a person become a disciple of Jesus Christ because of a decision to believe or because of a lifestyle of obedience? In a real sense, both answers are correct and shouldn't be separated from each other. Those who truly believe will want to obey, and those who are committed to obeying realize they will only succeed because they believe.

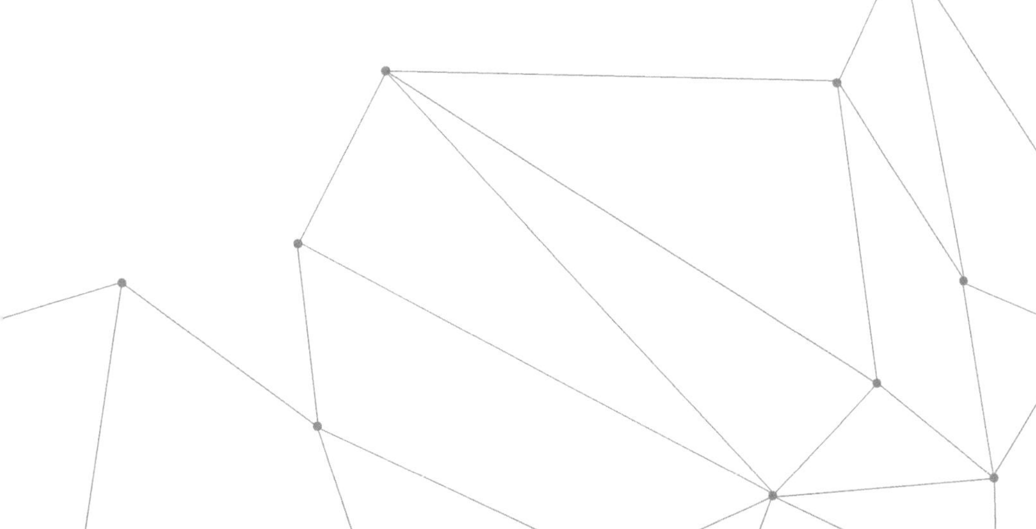

[ ] SUMMARY

We've seen how the story of the Bible is the story of a holy yet loving God who is on mission to spread his glory. He accomplishes this purpose by reconciling men and women to himself through his Son, Jesus Christ. This is truly good news. We become disciples of Jesus when we believe and respond to the good news, and we demonstrate that we are his disciples as we learn to obey him in all aspects of our lives. We engage in missions when we seek to fulfill God's command to make disciples of all nations.

FOR FURTHER DISCUSSION

We live in a needy world filled with suffering, pain and death. This raises the question, *"Does the command to make disciples include a responsibility to address these needs?"* When we understand that a disciple is one who imitates his master and we look closely at the life of Jesus, the answer is a very clear 'yes!' You can refer to these passages to see the importance God places on meeting human needs: Matthew 25:34–40; James 1:27; James 2:15–18.

So, the question isn't whether or not we are responsible to meet human needs. We are. Rather, the question is one of how to balance eternal spiritual needs with temporal physical needs. As someone recently observed, *"Certainly God cares about all human suffering, but especially about eternal suffering."*

Today many evangelical Christians are engaged in improving agriculture, fostering economic development, providing medicine, education, clean water, orphan care, and more.

Considering what we've learned, how might you encourage them to keep making disciples at the center of their efforts to bless others?

CHAPTER TWO

WHY STAYING HOME WAS NEVER AN OPTION

OVERVIEW:

We've established that Jesus wants us to prioritize making disciples, now let's dig a little deeper into our key passage. In this chapter, we'll explore how the early disciples were transformed into witnesses, as well as how they learned to overcome a series of significant obstacles. We'll also learn about recent progress in missions, and reflect upon the current imbalance in our efforts to make disciples of all nations.

VIDEO **bit.ly/TheStateOfTheWorld**

Questions for Discussion:

1. What did you like about the video?

2. What did you learn that is new to you?

INTRODUCTION:

A key word repeated throughout this video is access. The goal of dividing the seven billion people of our world into clusters A, B and C is to help us think about levels of access to the Good News.

Once we take this step, it quickly becomes clear that our efforts to make disciples are not equally distributed across the world. How might we address this inequality?

Our key passage addresses this inequality with the simple command: GO!

> *Go therefore and make disciples of all nations, baptizing them in the name of the Father and of the Son and of the Holy Spirit, teaching them to observe all that I have commanded you. And behold, I am with you always, to the end of the age.*
>
> **Jesus, quoted in Matthew 28:16–20**

How did the early disciples obey the command to go? What obstacles did they face? What can we learn from their example?

For help in answering these questions, we can turn to an early disciple named Luke. A physician by trade, Luke also served as the church's first historian. As a traveling companion of the apostle Paul, he conducted careful research that enabled him to write an accurate account of the life of Jesus and the early church. That history is captured in the books of Luke and Acts.

For our purposes, we'll focus specifically on how Luke describes the events that transformed the early disciples from mere followers into disciple-makers.

1. FROM TIMID FOLLOWERS TO POWERFUL WITNESSES

A. Before he released them to go, Jesus commanded the early disciples to stay.

> *Then [Jesus] said to them, "These are my words that I spoke to you while I was still with you, that everything written about me in the Law of Moses and the Prophets and the Psalms must be fulfilled." Then he opened their minds to understand the Scriptures, and said to them, "Thus it is written, that the Christ should suffer and on the third day rise from the dead, and that repentance for the forgiveness of sins should be proclaimed in his name to all nations, beginning from Jerusalem. You are witnesses of these things. And behold, I am sending the promise of my Father upon you. But stay in the city until you are clothed with power from on high."*
>
> **Luke 24:44–49**

This encounter took place after Jesus' resurrection and before his return to heaven. In just a few words, he clearly summarizes the central message of the Old Testament. Then he reminds them of the unique role they will fulfill as eyewitnesses of his death, burial and resurrection. He concludes by informing them that they're not ready to go because they're not yet *"clothed with power from on high."*

B. Jesus links the gift of the Holy Spirit to the ability to carry his message to the ends of the earth.

> *But you will receive power when the Holy Spirit has come upon you, and you will be my witnesses in Jerusalem and in all Judea and Samaria, and to the end of the earth." And when he had said these things, as they were looking on, he was lifted up, and a cloud took him out of their sight.*

Acts 1:8,9

In this passage, Jesus is only moments away from returning to his Father, and he explains in greater detail what he meant with the words, "*Go therefore and make disciples of all nations.*" His disciples must be willing to travel, moving outward in concentric circles from Jerusalem through Judea and Samaria to the most remote places on planet Earth.

However, they're not quite ready to be released. "*But you will receive power...*" is a clear reminder that something important is missing! Over the next ten days, the disciples would gather in a small room to wait and pray... and then came Pentecost!

C. Through the Holy Spirit, the disciples were transformed into powerful witnesses.

> *When the day of Pentecost arrived, they were all together in one place. And suddenly there came from heaven a sound like a mighty rushing wind, and it filled the entire house where they were sitting. And divided tongues as of fire appeared to them and rested on each one of them. And they were all filled with the Holy Spirit and began to speak in other tongues as the Spirit gave them utterance. Now there were dwelling in Jerusalem Jews, devout men from every nation under heaven. And at this*

sound the multitude came together, and they were bewildered, because each one was hearing them speak in his own language. And they were amazed and astonished, saying, "Are not all these who are speaking Galileans? And how is it that we hear, each of us in his own native language? Parthians and Medes and Elamites and residents of Mesopotamia, Judea and Cappadocia, Pontus and Asia, Phrygia and Pamphylia, Egypt and the parts of Libya belonging to Cyrene, and visitors from Rome, both Jews and proselytes, Cretans and Arabians—we hear them telling in our own tongues the mighty works of God." And all were amazed and perplexed, saying to one another, "What does this mean?" But others mocking said, "They are filled with new wine."

Acts 2:1–13

The miraculous signs that accompanied the arrival of the Holy Spirit were a fulfillment of Old Testament prophecies and a clear announcement that God was doing something new. Similar signs would occur at least two more times to demonstrate that the gift of the Holy Spirit is not confined to the first converts (see Acts 10:44–48; 19:5–7). While Acts 2:1–13 includes many important truths, for our purposes we want to focus on the main thing:

With the arrival of the Holy Spirit, the early disciples were transformed into powerful witnesses. In an instant, they moved from the defensive posture of waiting (and hiding) to the proactive posture of publicly proclaiming the Good News of Jesus Christ.

Today we understand that the Holy Spirit is a gift given to all true disciples of Jesus Christ the moment they become his followers. In other words, we don't need to wait for his arrival (see 1 Corinthians 12:13). For us, the issue is whether we access his power to speak fearlessly and clearly of our faith in Christ.

D. After the arrival of the Holy Spirit, the disciples traveled (although reluctantly at first) to the ends of the Earth.

FAST FACTS

Over the previous several hundred years, many Jews had scattered across the known world in search of a better life. Like immigrants throughout history, their children grew up 'between two worlds,' learning the local language and customs as well as the language and customs of their parents. They attracted some non-Jews to their religion, who were called proselytes. Many Jews and proselytes had the goal of making a pilgrimage to Jerusalem to worship in the Temple. This explains why there was such a variety of languages and people groups gathered in Jerusalem for the Feast of Pentecost.

And there arose on that day a great persecution against the church in Jerusalem, and they were all scattered throughout the regions of Judea and Samaria, except the apostles.

Acts 8:1

Now those who were scattered because of the persecution that arose over Stephen traveled as far as Phoenicia and Cyprus and Antioch, speaking the word to no one except Jews. But there were some of them, men of Cyprus and Cyrene, who on coming to Antioch spoke to the Hellenists also [non-Jews who spoke Greek], preaching the Lord Jesus. And the hand of the Lord was with them, and a great number who believed turned to the Lord.

Acts 11:19–21

These passages serve as an important reminder to us. While the early disciples had a clear command to go, and while they had the power to preach the good news, they preferred to stay close to home and witness to people who shared their language and culture. How did God address this problem? With a healthy dose of persecution! The remaining chapters of the book of Acts and the Epistles recount the story of the missionary expansion of the early church from Jerusalem to Rome and beyond.

QUESTIONS FOR DISCUSSION:

These passages from Luke and Acts clearly demonstrate the critically important role of the Holy Spirit. Without the courage and wisdom he provided, it is a safe assumption that the early disciples would have had little success in making disciples of all nations. Take a few moments to reflect upon the role of the Holy Spirit in our lives today. As we face the daunting task of making disciples, what should we ask and expect from the Holy Spirit?

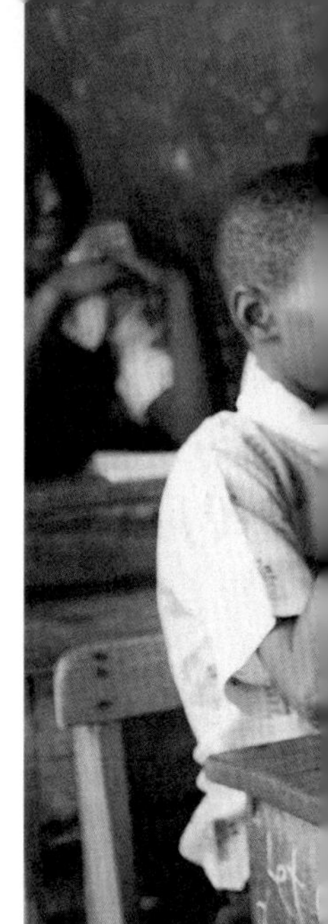

2. FROM DISCIPLES WHO PREFERRED HOME TO MISSIONARIES THAT WENT TO THE ENDS OF THE EARTH

This is a good moment to introduce our definition of missions:

Missions is the task of crossing barriers of language, geography, cultural differences and even prejudice to invite the nations to become true worshipers of God through Jesus Christ.

Perhaps an even simpler definition of missions is *crossing barriers to make disciples*. What are some of the most common barriers, and how did the early disciples overcome them?

A. The first major barrier to cross was language.

To demonstrate that language would not be a barrier to the gospel, the Holy Spirit gave to the early apostles the ability to speak in other languages.

> *Now there were dwelling in Jerusalem Jews, devout men from every nation under heaven. And at this sound the multitude came together, and they were bewildered, because each one was hearing them speak in his own language. And they were amazed and astonished, saying, "Are not all these who are speaking Galileans? And how is it that we hear, each of us in his own native language?*
>
> **Acts 2:5–8**

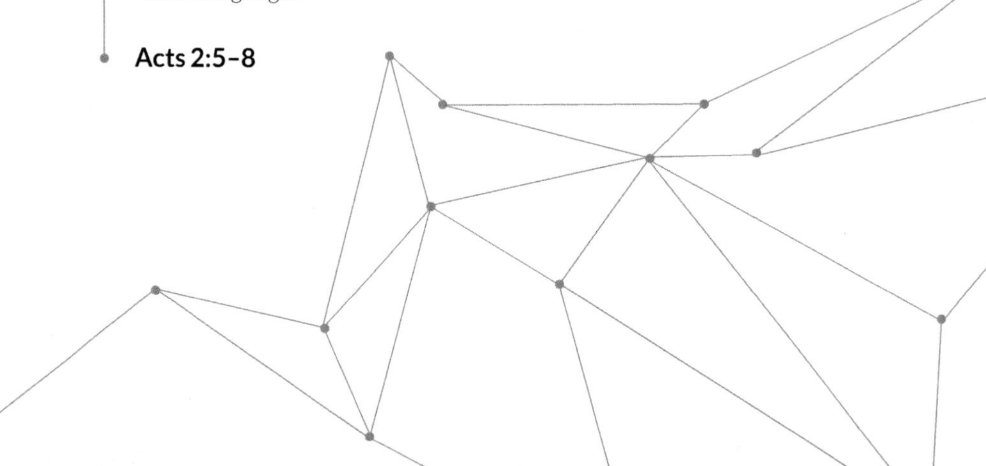

B. The second major barrier to cross was geography.

As we saw earlier, the Holy Spirit sent a great persecution against the early disciples to scatter them among the nations.

> *And there arose on that day a great persecution against the church in Jerusalem, and they were all scattered throughout the regions of Judea and Samaria, except the apostles.*
>
> **Acts 8:1**

C. The third major barrier to cross was ethnic prejudice.

Most people harbor a deep-seated belief of the superiority of their ethnic line. This was especially true of the Jewish nation. Acts 10:1–11,18 tells the story of how the Apostle Peter overcame his personal biases against non-Jews and embraced the reality that the gospel is good news for all peoples.

> *So Peter opened his mouth and said: "Truly I understand that God shows no partiality, but in every nation anyone who fears him and does what is right is acceptable to him."*
>
> **Acts 10:34,35**

D. The fourth major barrier cultural preferences.

As early Christians made disciples among the non-Jews, some suggested that these new believers should be required to observe the ceremonial laws and customs of the Jewish people. Acts 15:1–35 describes how leaders met in a great council to debate the issue. They concluded that other ethnic groups should be free to worship God using their own cultural forms, as long as these forms did not violate Scripture.

No! We believe it is through the grace of our Lord Jesus that we are saved, just as they are.

The apostle Peter in Acts 15:11

Therefore my judgment is that we should not trouble those of the Gentiles (read: nations) who turn to God."

The elder James in Acts 15:19

QUESTIONS FOR DISCUSSION:

Let's take a moment to reflect upon these four barriers to making disciples of all nations. In your opinion, which barriers might be easier for us to overcome today? Which barriers remain more difficult? Why?

WORTH PONDERING:

Over the past 2,000 years, we've made significant progress toward the goal of making disciples of all nations. Yet, as our video pointed out, most missionaries and finances today are focused on making disciples in regions of the world where many churches and believers already exist.

The missionary task is fundamentally that of crossing barriers to take the good news where it isn't. Certainly local churches in World B and World C are responsible to make disciples in their immediate communities. We call this outreach. But what about World A? What will it take for us to truly embrace our responsibility to cross barriers with the good news? Are we willing to 'go?'

We've focused on the responsibilities and challenges related to the command to go. We discovered how the early disciples were not ready to go until they received the gift of the Holy Spirit, a gift that all of us receive today when we believe in Jesus Christ. The power and wisdom available to us through the Holy Spirit is indispensable in our quest to make disciples of all nations. We also discovered the primary obstacles early disciples overcame as they moved out in concentric circles from Jerusalem to Rome and beyond. We face similar obstacles today. Making disciples of all nations requires us to leave what is close, comfortable and familiar.

FOR FURTHER DISCUSSION

There is a tendency in some circles today to label everything we do in Jesus' name as missions, and to call every Christian a missionary. While every true disciple of Jesus Christ is commanded to make disciples, we prefer to reserve the terms mission and missionary to those who cross significant barriers. Because of our study today, how do you feel about these terms? Do you see any value in drawing a distinction between what we do locally (outreach) and cross-culturally (missions)? Why or why not?

CHAPTER THREE

WHY WE FOCUS ON NATIONS

OVERVIEW:

We now turn to the central place that nations occupy in God's eternal plan. From Genesis through Revelation and beyond, we discover that God created the nations, loves the nations, and intends for the nations to form an important part of the 'eternal landscape.' But how can we ensure that the disciples we help make among every nation will grow to maturity in Christ, and continue the quest to make more disciples? By gathering those disciples into healthy, culturally-relevant local churches.

INTRODUCTION:

Let's begin by reviewing our key passage, and the main lessons we've learned so far:

> *Go therefore and make disciples of all nations, baptizing them in the name of the Father and of the Son and of the Holy Spirit, teaching them to observe all that I have commanded you. And behold, I am with you always, to the end of the age.*
>
> **Jesus, quoted in Matthew 28:16–20**

In Chapter One, we discovered that the task of missions is the task of making disciples of all nations. We learned that genuine disciples respond in belief to truth about Jesus Christ, and they commit to a lifetime of learning to obey all his commands. This process takes time, so our commitment to missions needs to be a long-term commitment. Also, the video introduced us to the origin and eternal destiny of the nations, a topic we'll continue to develop.

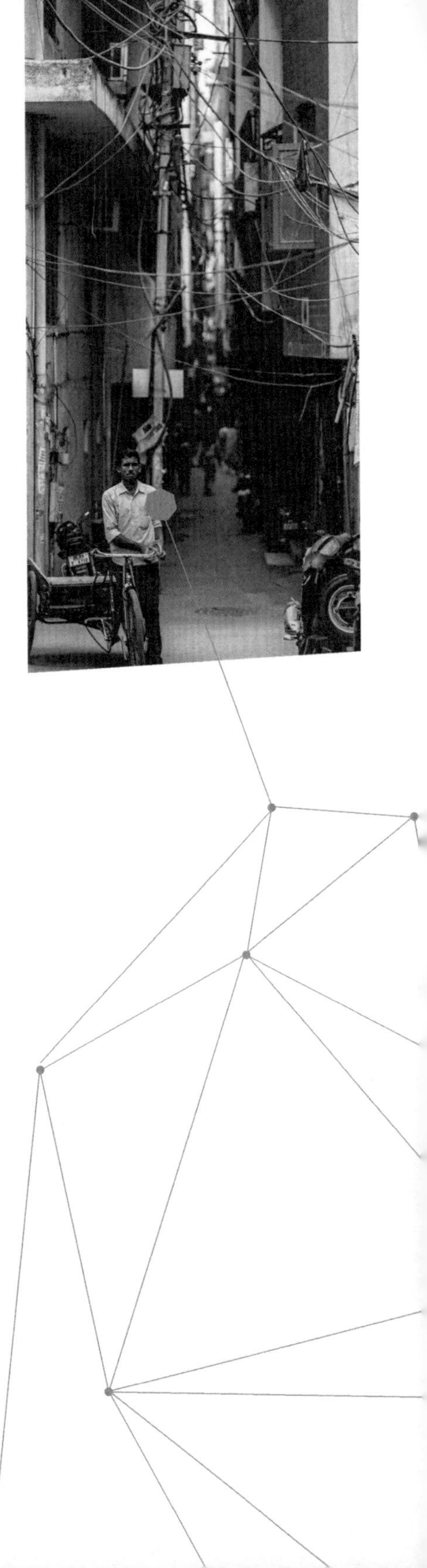

In Chapter Two, we focused on our responsibility to go. For the early disciples, this required them to leave what was comfortable and familiar. At great personal sacrifice, they shared the good news in concentric circles radiating out from Jerusalem to Rome and beyond. We examined four obstacles they overcame, and reflected upon how missions requires us to overcome similar obstacles today. Through the video, we learned how there are still large regions of the world where men and women have very limited access to the good news.

In this chapter we turn our focus to two important topics that will help complete our basic understanding of missions: who and where are all nations, and what is the role of local churches in developing a sustainable ministry of disciple-making among all nations?

DIGGING DEEPER

In the original language of the New Testament, the words translated all nations are panta ta ethne. We include them here to draw your attention to the word ethne, from which we receive our modern English word ethnic. Another appropriate translation is the term *people group*. In missions, we define a people group as:

A culturally homogeneous group of people who share a common language, institutions, religion and history.

We believe this definition of people group or nation is consistent with the meaning of the term ethne in Scripture. Unfortunately, many people tend to respond to ethnic differences in one of two ways. Either they delight in learning about cultural differences and sampling ethnic foods, or they see these differences as a threat to their own security and well-being.

FAST FACTS

As late as 2014, the U.S. immigrant population stood at more than 42.4 million, or 13.3%, of the total U.S. population of 318.9 million. Between 2013 and 2014, the foreign-born population increased by 1 million, or 2.5%. Immigrants in the United States and their U.S.-born children now number approximately 81 million people, or 26% of the overall U.S. population.[1]

[1] Source: http://www.migrationpolicy.org/article/frequently-requested-statistics-immigrants-and-immigration-united-states (consulted Dec 2016)

QUESTIONS FOR DISCUSSION:

If you were to share that FAST FACT with various people you know, how might they respond? Would they see the influx of new people groups into the USA in a positive or negative light? Why? What might their responses reveal about attitudes toward those whose ethnic origins are different from their own?

1. GOD IS AT WORK AMONG THE NATIONS TO RECONCILE MEN AND WOMEN TO HIMSELF

> *The God who made the world and everything in it, being Lord of heaven and earth, does not live in temples made by man, nor is he served by human hands, as though he needed anything, since he himself gives to all mankind life and breath and everything. And he made from one man every nation of mankind to live on all the face of the earth, having determined allotted periods and the boundaries of their dwelling place, that they should seek God, and perhaps feel their way toward him and find him. Yet he is actually not far from each one of us.*
>
> **The apostle Paul, quoted in Acts 17:24–27**

Among the many important truths in this passage, we clearly see that the nations are not an accident, nor are they a curiosity. Rather, they form an integral part of God's plan to bring salvation to the world. God created the nations, God determines when and where they inhabit the earth, and, in ways that go beyond our comprehension, God uses ethnic diversity to call men and women to himself.

VIDEO **bit.ly/WhatIsAUPG**

This video does an excellent job of helping us better understand the nations, and helps define the finish line for the missionary task.

Questions for Discussion:

1. What did you like about the video?

2. What did you learn that is new to you?

A commitment to making disciples of all nations requires us to think in terms of the 16,000 ethnic groups that inhabit our world today. Who are they? Where do they live? What degree of access do they have to the good news? Is anyone currently doing missions work or planning to do missions work among them? We believe we have a responsibility to prioritize our limited resources (personnel and finances) to help ensure that there is a viable church among every people group. Among nations where churches already exist, we call upon those churches to rise up and embrace their own responsibility to make disciples among their own people.

> *It has always been my ambition to preach the gospel where Christ was not known, so that I would not be building on someone else's foundation.*
>
> **The apostle Paul in Romans 15:20 (NIV)**

Up to this point, we've focused almost exclusively on how the words of Jesus in Matthew 28:19,20 help us better understand the task of missions. This famous passage is often referred to as the Great Commission. But there's another, equally significant responsibility Jesus entrusted to us. The early disciples embraced it, as have all those who throughout history have taken the Great Commission seriously. We're referring to the need to gather new believers into healthy, culturally relevant local churches.

2. GOD USES LOCAL CHURCHES TO SUSTAIN DISCIPLE-MAKING EFFORTS AMONG THE NATIONS.

A. The church is central to Jesus' plan for this age. Even before commanding his early followers to make disciples, Jesus announced his plan to build his church:

I will build my church, and the gates of hell shall not prevail against it.

Jesus, quoted in Matthew 16:18

FAST FACTS

While it is impossible to have exact statistics, our best research indicates that there may be as many as 7,000 people groups with less than 2% evangelical presence. In practical terms, this means that unless someone engages in missionary work it is highly unlikely that we will see significant progress in reaching that group. If you have more interest in learning about the world's people groups, we encourage you to consult with these resources:

- joshuaproject.net
- finishingthetask.com

B. The church serves as the ideal place to nurture new disciples and encourage them toward growth and fruitfulness.

And they [read: the church] devoted themselves to the apostles' teaching and the fellowship, to the breaking of bread and the prayers. And awe came upon every soul, and many wonders and signs were being done through the apostles. And all who believed were together and had all things in common. And they were selling their possessions and belongings and distributing the proceeds to all, as any had need. And day by day, attending the temple together and breaking bread in their homes, they received their food with glad and generous hearts, praising God and having favor with all the people. And the Lord added to their number day by day those who were being saved.

Acts 2:42–47

C. Through the church, Jesus exercises the power to bring about reconciliation between people from different ethnic backgrounds.

Therefore remember that at one time you Gentiles [read: nations]…were at that time separated from Christ, alienated from the commonwealth of Israel and strangers to the covenants of promise, having no hope and without God in the world. But now in Christ Jesus you who once were far off have been brought near by the blood of Christ. For he himself is our peace, who has made us both one and has broken down in his flesh the dividing wall of hostility by abolishing the law of commandments expressed in ordinances, that he might create in himself one new man [read: church] in place of the two, so making peace, and might reconcile us both to God in one body through the cross, thereby killing the hostility.

Ephesians 2:11–16

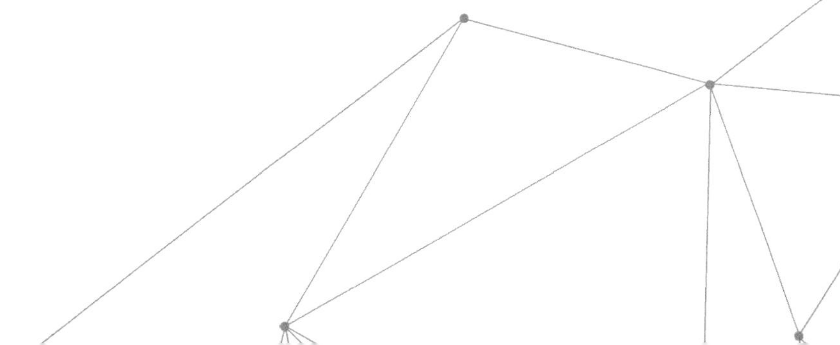

We should not be surprised that the early disciples placed a high priority on gathering men and women into churches wherever they succeeded in making disciples. In fact, the idea that a disciple would not join a local church is completely foreign to the New Testament.

These truths help explain why healthy churches place special emphasis on disciple-making activities that help start and strengthen local churches among the nations. When selecting people and projects to support, churches may prioritize efforts that will ultimately help establish strong and culturally sensitive local churches.

3. FOR CHURCHES TO BE EFFECTIVE AMONG THE NATIONS, THEY MUST BE CULTURALLY RELEVANT.

Let's take a moment to reflect once again on the example of the early disciples. Do you remember the church council we mentioned in the previous chapter? It might be easy to overlook the implications of Acts 15, but that historic precedent impacts effective missions work today.

It's a common human tendency to assume that our culture is superior to others, and that the way we do things is the way they ought to be done. Stated in another way, all of us tend to wear 'cultural blinders' that make it difficult for us to accept the validity of how other cultures think and act. We're not referring to customs that clearly violate Scripture, but rather to our multitude of preferences. If we're not careful, we can easily fall into the trap of concluding that our way is the only way.

This reality has huge implications for missions. If we're honest with ourselves and with history, we'll see that good churches have flourished in many parts of the world with significant differences in the way they worshipped God and organized their activities. The churches we establish in other cultures ought to look different from ours. This means that every missionary faces the challenge of separating between the essence of the church as described in the New Testament, and his or her own cultural expressions of the church. The goal is to gather new disciples into healthy, culturally relevant churches. Another way to express this tension is:

In missions, we commit to planting the seed (essence) of the church in the diverse cultural soils of our world, as opposed to transplanting our model of church.

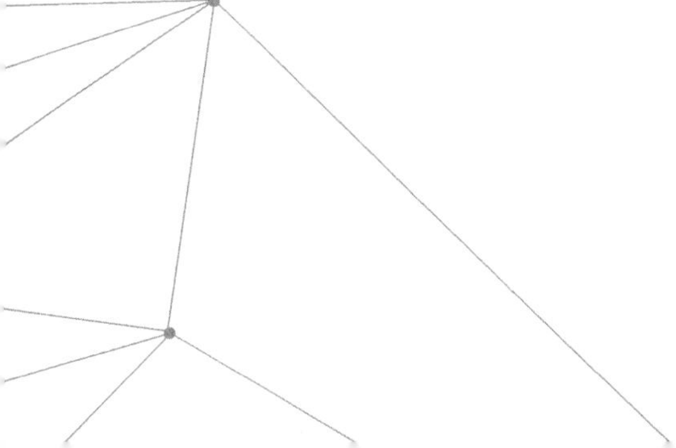

QUESTIONS FOR DISCUSSION:

Let's imagine you're invited to visit a church among a people group very different than your own. Afterwards, the local missionary asks, "What do you think?" What criteria might you use to evaluate whether or not this church is strong and culturally relevant? What we've observed about the need to adapt a church to the unique cultural soil where it's planted also applies to the very methods and materials we employ to make disciples in the first place. In missions, we call this process *contextualization.*

> *Contextualization is the commitment to apply the unchanging truth of God's Word in a specific cultural setting in a way that removes unnecessary barriers to understanding and acceptance.*

WORTH PONDERING:

By now, we hope you're developing a deeper appreciation for some of the principal challenges to making disciples among the world's diverse people groups. The missionary task is far more complex than simply translating a short gospel presentation from our language to another. It requires a sincere commitment to 1) discovering how people think, 2) learning to express truth in their language and cultural forms, and 3) staying long enough to see tangible results—new disciples of Jesus Christ gathered into strong and culturally relevant churches. No wonder the final words of Jesus are so important:

> *And behold, I am with you always, to the end of the age.*
>
> **Jesus, quoted in Matthew 28:20**

[ ] SUMMARY

In our quest to help you have a well-rounded introduction to missions, we've focused this chapter on three big challenges:

1 // prioritizing our efforts among the nations that have little access to the good news,

2 // ensuring that new disciples are gathered into healthy local churches, and

3 // learning to adapt our methods (contextualize) to remove unnecessary barriers.

FOR FURTHER DISCUSSION

This chapter's video presented an easy way to help us remember the world's least-reached peoples using the acrostic THUMB. Can you remember what each letter represents?

What do you know about these major religious clusters? Select the group that you know most about. Then brainstorm concerning some of the unique challenges a missionary might face in sharing the good news among one of the nations that forms part of this religious cluster. Does this exercise help you grow in your appreciation for the hard work of contextualization?

CHAPTER FOUR

HOW CAN I GET INVOLVED?

OVERVIEW:

After a short review of what we've learned in previous sessions, we conclude our study by answering the important questions *"How is your local church obeying Jesus' command to make disciples of all nations?"* and *"How can I get involved?"* We'll discover that there are four basic ways every man, woman and child can engage in missions, and we'll explain how your church is creating paths you can follow towards the fulfillment of the Great Commission.

INTRODUCTION:

Let's begin by reviewing our key passage, and the main lessons we've learned so far:

> *Go therefore and make disciples of all nations, baptizing them in the name of the Father and of the Son and of the Holy Spirit, teaching them to observe all that I have commanded you. And behold, I am with you always, to the end of the age.*
>
> **Jesus, quoted in Matthew 28:16–20**

WHAT HAVE WE LEARNED TO THIS POINT?

CHAPTER ONE:

One Priority

The Bible is the story of God revealing his glory to all mankind. He invites us into that story by commissioning us to make disciples of Jesus Christ among all nations. A *disciple* is a *learner* or *follower* who begins his or her journey by believing certain truths which we summarize with the terms *gospel*, or *good news*. A disciple also commits to a lifestyle of *learning to obey all Jesus commanded us*. We might ask, "Does a person become a disciple of Jesus Christ because of a decision to believe or because of a lifestyle of obedience?" In a real sense, both answers are correct and shouldn't be separated from each other. Those who truly believe will want to obey, and those committed to obeying realize they will only succeed because they truly believe. Our one priority is to make disciples of Jesus Christ among all nations!

CHAPTER TWO:

Why staying home was never an option

With the arrival of the Holy Spirit, the early disciples abandoned the defensive posture of waiting (and hiding) and publicly proclaimed the good news of Jesus Christ. Today we receive the same Spirit the moment we become followers of Christ, but we must learn to access his power to speak fearlessly and clearly of our faith in Jesus. Also, while powerful witnesses in their own communities, the early disciples struggled to overcome several barriers that impeded the spread of the good news to the ends of the earth. We face the same obstacles today. Missions is the task of crossing barriers of language, geography, cultural differences and even prejudice to invite the nations to become true worshipers of God through Jesus Christ.

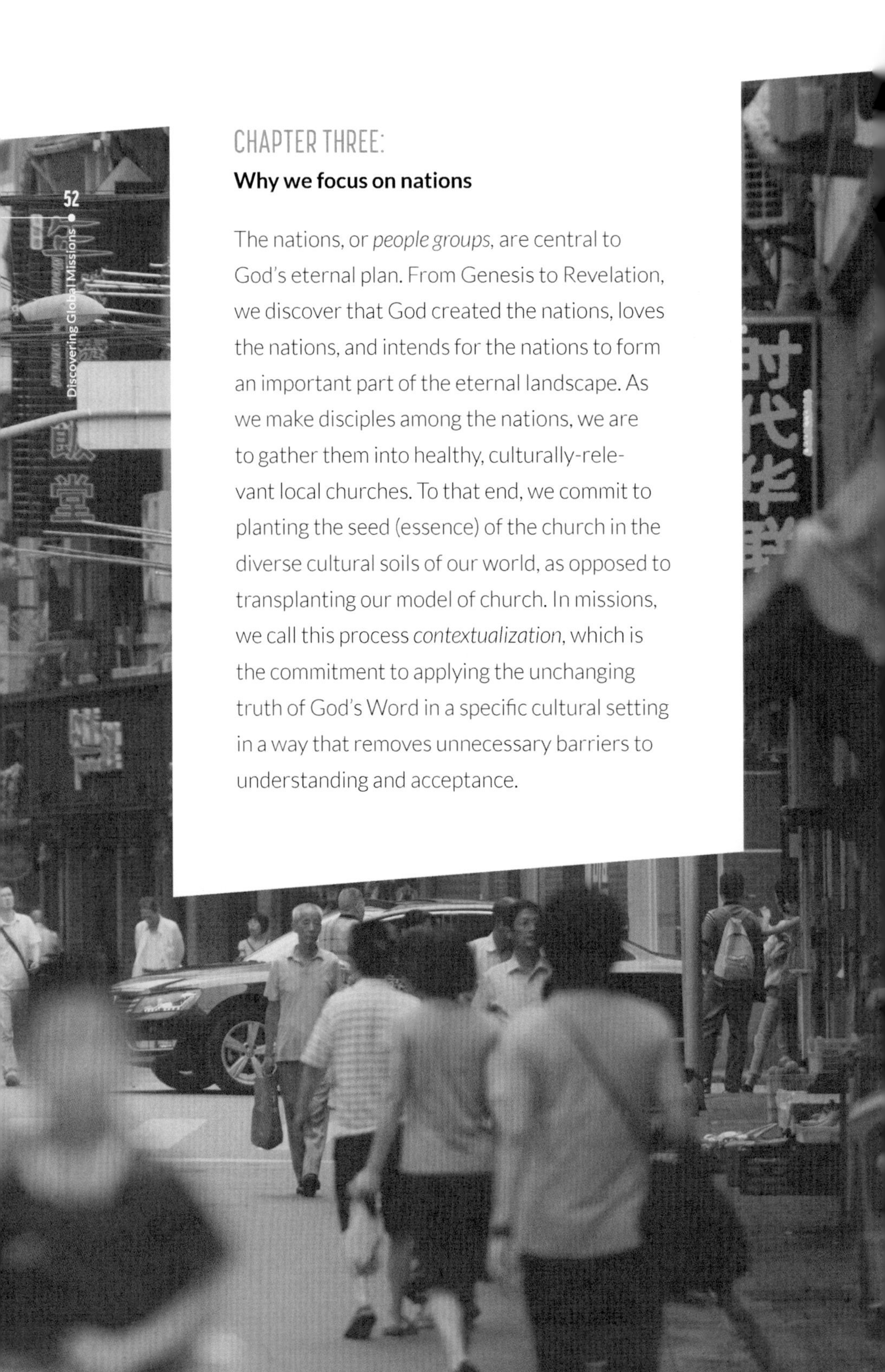

CHAPTER THREE:

Why we focus on nations

The nations, or *people groups*, are central to God's eternal plan. From Genesis to Revelation, we discover that God created the nations, loves the nations, and intends for the nations to form an important part of the eternal landscape. As we make disciples among the nations, we are to gather them into healthy, culturally-relevant local churches. To that end, we commit to planting the seed (essence) of the church in the diverse cultural soils of our world, as opposed to transplanting our model of church. In missions, we call this process *contextualization*, which is the commitment to applying the unchanging truth of God's Word in a specific cultural setting in a way that removes unnecessary barriers to understanding and acceptance.

Now that we've established a basic understanding of missions, what are the specific pathways our church creates so that every person can get involved?

1. THROUGH PRAYING

> *And even if our gospel is veiled, it is veiled to those who are perishing.In their case the god of this world has blinded the minds of the unbelievers, to keep them from seeing the light of the gospel of the glory of Christ, who is the image of God.*
>
> **2 Corinthians 4:3,4**

> *Continue steadfastly in prayer, being watchful in it with thanksgiving. At the same time, pray also for us, that God may open to us a door for the word, to declare the mystery of Christ, on account of which I am in prison—that I may make it clear, which is how I ought to speak.*
>
> **Colossians 4:2–4**

WHAT ARE SOME OF THE WAYS YOUR CHURCH MOBILIZES PEOPLE TO PRAY?

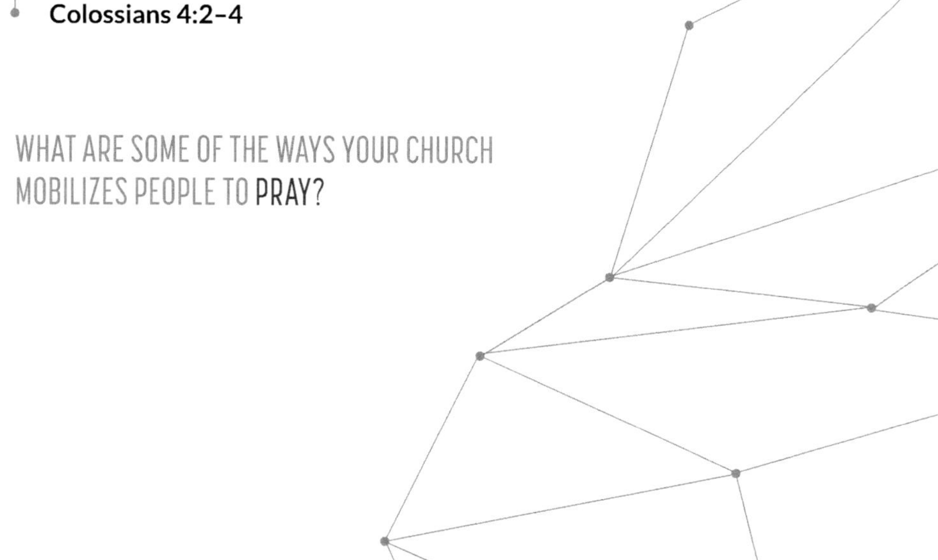

2. THROUGH GIVING

Beloved, it is a faithful thing you do in all your efforts for these brothers,strangers as they are, who testified to your love before the church. You will do well to send them on their journey in a manner worthy of God.

3 John 5,6

For they have gone out for the sake of the name, accepting nothing from the Gentiles. Therefore we ought to support people like these, that we may be fellow workers for the truth.

3 John 7,8

WHAT ARE SOME OF THE WAYS YOUR CHURCH MOBILIZES PEOPLE TO GIVE?

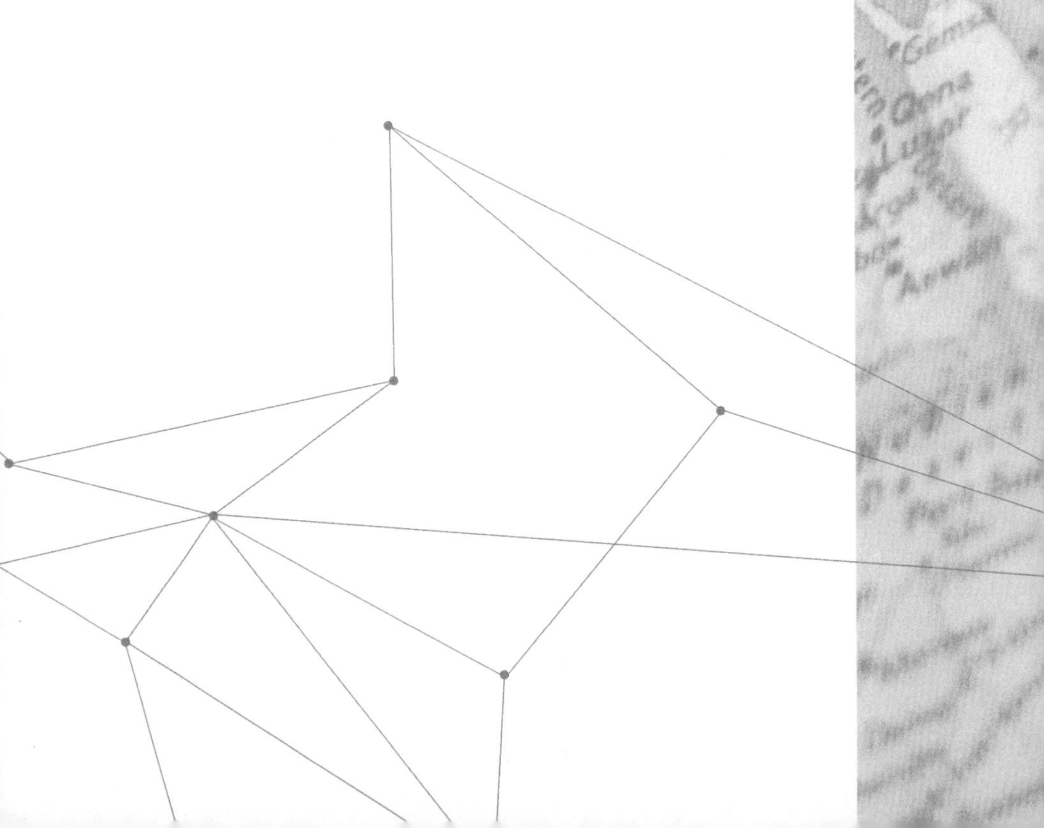

3. THROUGH GOING

> *In the church at Antioch there were prophets and teachers: Barnabas, Simeon called Niger, Lucius of Cyrene, Manaen (who had been brought up with Herod the tetrarch) and Saul. While they were worshiping the Lord and fasting, the Holy Spirit said, "Set apart for me Barnabas and Saul for the work to which I have called them." So after they had fasted and prayed, they placed their hands on them and sent them off ('set free,' 'released'). The two of them, sent on their way by the Holy Spirit, went down to Seleucia and sailed from there to Cyprus.*
>
> **Acts 13:1–4**

WHAT ARE SOME OF THE WAYS YOUR CHURCH MOBILIZES PEOPLE TO GO?

VIDEO **bit.ly/GodsHeartForTheForeigner**

Questions for Discussion:

1. What did you like about the video?

2. What did you learn that is new to you?

4. THROUGH WELCOMING

And [God] made from one man every nation of mankind to live on all the face of the earth, having determined allotted periods and the boundaries of their dwelling place, that they should seek God, and perhaps feel their way toward him and find him.

Acts 17:26,27

WHAT ARE SOME OF THE WAYS YOUR CHURCH MOBILIZES PEOPLE TO WELCOME THE NATIONS AMONG US?

PERSONAL SUMMARY:

Take a moment to review the material we've covered in this study on missions. Can you identify three things you've learned?

1.

2.

3.

NEXT STEPS:

Now take a moment to review what you've learned in this chapter about the opportunities your church is creating to help you engage in praying, giving, going and welcoming. Can you identify at least two opportunities and the next steps you plan to take to pursue them?

1.

2.

CONCLUSION:

Congratulations on completing *Discovering Global Missions*! We trust you've learned something useful AND that you intend to put it into practice. We urge you to pursue one or more of the paths to missions' engagement within your local church!

DISCOVERING GLOBAL MISSIONS is designed to *bring clarity that produces participation* with respect to the missions priorities of your local church. In a day when *missions* is defined by many competing voices, these studies take us back to the best possible sources of information and inspiration—Jesus Christ and his early disciples. We focus on allowing the New Testament to lead us to a deeper understanding and appreciation of key concepts like making disciples, the essence of the Good News, the indispensable role of the Holy Spirit, overcoming the primary obstacles for missions, the role of contextualization and the necessity of establishing healthy and culturally relevant churches. We conclude by offering you the opportunity to explain how your church is mobilizing for missions and to invite participants to take concrete steps toward engagement.

HERE ARE FOUR THINGS YOU NEED TO KNOW:

1. PROVIDING COPIES OF THE BOOK

Each participant will need their own copy of the book. These can be purchased at Amazon.com

2. LEADING THROUGH THE BOOK

This material is designed for both individual and group use. Depending on your class and teaching style, you must decide whether it's best to teach the material or simply to ask participants to read the paragraphs out loud, followed by your comments.

3. ACCESSING VIDEOS

Each session includes a video, courtesy of our friends at Global Frontier Missions. You can access all four videos at bit.ly/DiscoveringGlobalMissions.

4. PREPARING FOR CHAPTER FOUR: HOW CAN I GET INVOLVED?

The final chapter will require careful preparation. This is your opportunity to present a summary of the specific ways that your local church to encourages praying, giving, going, and welcoming the nations to your community. We urge you to be clear, concise, and to provide concrete "next steps!"

Made in the USA
San Bernardino, CA
08 July 2019